PRAISE FOR *The Largeness of Rescue*

The Largeness of Rescue is a book of bot [illegible]
ing for clarity and a reconciliation. In this way, the poems form a moving whole, seeking resolution in the larger embrace of art.
—Anne Michaels, author of *Fugitive Pieces* and *The Winter Vault*

With clarity and insight, Eva Tihanyi's poetry offers both personal revelation and mature reflection on art, time and history. Serene in spirit and precise in language, *The Largeness of Rescue* is her finest work.
—Carole Giangrande, author of *Here Comes the Dreamer* and *Midsummer*

Long-time readers of Eva Tihanyi's powerful poetry have always appreciated her clarity and candor. Now, in her eighth collection, *The Largeness of Rescue*, we see the poet's deep reckoning with loss, longing and mortality. Whether it's a student crying in her office, or the slow demise of jazz genius Chet Baker, or the poets Byron, Keats, and Shelley in Italy, Tihanyi's soulful poems show an intimate understanding of life—and often the great human cost of art. Tihanyi offers us poetry that whispers from one heart to another.
—Bruce Hunter, author of *Two O'clock Creek: Poems New and Selected* and *In the Bear's House*

The Largeness of Rescue is a grave and tender collection, much preoccupied with issues of choice and destiny, and how they resonate throughout our lives. "Is it a tragedy when you choose?" she asks of the self-destructive jazz genius Chet Baker, and envisions T .S. Eliot turning his back on the "bad Russian novel" of his life to "foray into literature / on a plank of contrived neutrality / which he himself does not trust." Most of the personae of these poems are nameless and their struggles and regrets less celebrated, but no less resonant: having been laughed at at twelve for his clumsiness, a man refuses to dance, in later years, with the wife who loves dancing, so that "Eventually / no one is dancing." What connects them all is an awareness of life's central paradox: we are always hoping to arrive somewhere better, even though all we have is the present moment.
—Susan Glickman, author of *Safe as Houses* and *Running in Prospect Cemetery: New and Selected Poems*

Eva Tihanyi's *The Largeness of Rescue* explores the many ways we both long for and resist rescue—rescue from ourselves, from each other, from the vagaries of the world. These poems sit poised at the cusp of a paradox, that place between "hope and hopelessness," "horror and wonder" ("Precept") where the personal explodes into the public realm. "I" becomes "you" becomes "we." This is a book about borders, about "the middle place of possibility" that can move us past "carrion fear." Tihanyi's cycle contains both shorter lyrics and long poems, some of which explore the lives of artists and visionaries whose work sustained a precarious creativity: the Romantic poets, T.S. Eliot, and jazz trumpeter Chet Baker. Among these luminaries, also arise the poet's peers, family, friends, fellow artists, and loves. The book reveals how, not despite, but through our common uncertainties and frailties, we hold the power to rescue. Rescue becomes not only a noun but a verb. Choosing to become rescuers (each in our own small way) is in itself a means of rescue. In the end it is the heart's measure that proffers hope: "but always I will side with love / and always I will choose."
—Susan McCaslin, author of *Into the Mystic: My Years with Olga* and *Demeter Goes Skydiving*

Among my favorite poems in this reflective collection are those tributes Eva Tihanyi composes to the artist. There is her powerful evocation of Chet Baker and the "tendrils of melody" and charismatic notes" that emanate from his "brooding trumpet"; the complex mix of his giftedness, his inconsolability, the lure of fame and the prison of his addiction. Then too, she offers a rich portrait of T. S. Eliot, who struggled to "crack the code of his insurgent heart"; and before him, Tihanyi remembers the legacy of the Romantic Poets, the places they lived and their "allegiance to words," which can "ignite like a tiny sun." As she notes the particulars of all their lives, and the continuum of learning our own, Tihanyi asks that we pledge to live—to live in love—in spite of the paradoxes which fill this collection with subdued wonder.
—Carol Lipszyc, author of *The Saviour Shoes and Other Stories* and *Singing Me Home*

Eva Tihanyi writes with clarity by employing powerful metaphors and epigrammatic language with an unflinching philosophical honesty to capture the conditions of

our lives. If there is a dark atmosphere in some of these poems, there is also an underlying hope expressed in tender affirmation.
—Laurence Hutchman, author of *Personal Encounters* and *The Writers' Words: Conversations with Eight Canadian Poets*

"Art is not a closed circle / or a straight line." Eva Tihanyi's poems evoke many moments of art, from Chet Baker's music drifting from an Italian prison to a cave artist placing handprints on rock. She pieces these moments together along the curving trails of lyric and perception.
—Alice Major, author of *Standard Candles* and *Intersecting Sets: A Poet Looks at Science*

May 5, 2016

The LARGENESS of RESCUE

To Sonia —

Thank you for attending the launch. So nice to see you off FB.

:) Eva

Canada Council for the Arts Conseil des Arts du Canada

ONTARIO ARTS COUNCIL
CONSEIL DES ARTS DE L'ONTARIO
an Ontario government agency
un organisme du gouvernement de l'Ontario

Canada

The publisher gratefully acknowledges the support of the Canada Council for the Arts and the Ontario Arts Council for its publishing program. The publisher is also grateful for the financial assistance received from the Government of Canada through the Canada Book Fund.

Front cover photograph: Stephen Orlando www.motionexposure.com

Cover design: Val Fullard

Library and Archives Canada Cataloguing in Publication

Tihanyi, Eva, 1956-, author
The largeness of rescue : poems / by Eva Tihanyi.

(Inanna poetry and fiction series)
Issued in print and electronic formats.
ISBN 978-1-77133-297-2 (paperback). -- ISBN 978-1-77133-298-9 (epub).-- ISBN 978-1-77133-300-9 (pdf)

I. Title. II. Series: Inanna poetry and fiction series

PS8589.I53L37 2016 C811'.54 C2016-900292-6
C2016-900293-4

MIX
Paper from responsible sources
FSC www.fsc.org FSC® C004071

Printed and bound in Canada

Inanna Publications and Education Inc.
210 Founders College, York University
4700 Keele Street, Toronto, Ontario M3J 1P3 Canada
Telephone: (416) 736-5356 Fax (416) 736-5765
Email: inanna.publications@inanna.ca Website: www.inanna.ca

The LARGENESS of RESCUE

POEMS BY

Eva Tihanyi

inanna poetry & fiction series

INANNA Publications and Education Inc.
Toronto, Canada

ALSO BY EVA TIHANYI

FICTION

Truth and Other Fictions

POETRY

Flying Underwater: Poems New and Selected

In the Key of Red

Wresting the Grace of the World

Restoring the Wickedness

Saved by the Telling

Prophecies Near the Speed of Light

A Sequence of the Blood

for Constance and for Brendan

Contents

The world asks of us
only the strength we have and we give it.
Then it asks more, and we give it.

—Jane Hirshfield

Psychic Readings

1.

Anything
can happen
to anyone
in any place
at any time.

And does.

2.

The essence of randomness:
an expectation of order.

3.

Soon you will find yourself
in front of the house
where your child was born
and so much else was borne.

And you will look up
at the window behind which
so often you stood

looking out to the street
where you now stand.

You must try to understand
what you are grieving.

4.

If you line up all the places
where you've lived, you will see
a map of your life.

Essential, that you learn
to navigate.

5.

There are longings
you hoard like heirlooms.

Let go of them.

6.

In the season of nesting
the anxious birds
will quest for twigs.

You too will search and build.

7.

Although heights terrify you,
you will climb a great tree.

The view will change you
but you will be stranded,
unable to come down.

Your greatest hope
will be rescue.

Your greatest fear
will be rescue also.

And Then We Are Faced With It

And then we are faced with it,
the immeasurable, the unforeseen,
the certain uncertainty.

We are not expecting this encounter,
at least not for a while, not today.
But it is always today.
There is nothing else though we pretend.

This is not magic, this toxic self-consciousness.
It murders the hours with mirrors and smoke,
the illusion of answers.

We want to know more,
we always want to know more.
So much for the sanity of ignorance.
It is not the human condition.

Try again, try harder.
Oblivion will come soon enough.

Circles and Lines

1.

July 31, 1960.

Chet Baker races toward Viareggio,
the late afternoon road uncoiling
like a languid serpent, the horizon
an illusion of certainty, his quest for home
a stubborn unacknowledged longing
without end or consolation.

Needs, wants, must have a fix.
Stops at a gas station in Lucca, locks
himself in the washroom,
does not reappear.

Time passes. The attendant knocks,
then bangs, keeps banging, eventually
assumes emergency.
When the police arrive,
they find a disheveled man
standing dazed before the blood-spattered sink
syringe in hand.

It will linger for days, the stench
of Paco Rabanne cologne and week-old sweat.

2.

Is it a tragedy when you choose?

3.

The trial eight months later
is sensational, the defendant
found guilty.

San Giorgio Penitentiary looms
at the centre of town, its medieval walls
and black windows as unrepentant
as its celebrity prisoner who, for years a vagrant
in his own life, is now jailed in it.

The second wife has been discarded,
the new mistress ensconced in the Hotel Universo,
the press duly scandalized.

Served: an Italian drama
of operatic proportions.

The world laps it up
like a thirsty dog.

4.

Before the arrest, a triumph:

Chet Baker plays Il Bussolotto,
a grand nightclub lounge on the Tyrrhenian Sea.

The patrons anoint him their *trombo d'oro*, adore
the intimate coolness of his jazz worship
in the summer air.

What they don't see:
how at the end of the night
he tosses his horn on the piano,
rushes out for the next fix.

How in the morning
the sun falls in
through the sea-facing picture window,
alights on the tarnished horn, such sad beauty.

5.

Art is not a closed circle
or a straight line.

The heart embraces its craving, the blood rises,
a great irrational wave washing over
the unsuspecting bones, and all is deluged
in its red tidings, the secret song divulged,
its rhythm, rhythm, rhythm
beating time into submission, beating time.

If this were true, it couldn't be said.

And to hold it: impossible
as a signature on water.

6.

Church bells and a lone trumpet—
the sounds of Lucca that summer
as the locals gather along the promenade
to hear "Someone to Watch Over Me"
in the evening stillness.

During the day Chet Baker plays chess,
waits for visits from his mistress
who waits for his release.
Even the air waits.

And every night the sound
of the brooding trumpet, tendrils of melody
curling and winding, climbing and falling,
tender above all.

7.

Flashback.

There is nothing as seductive as genius.
Women will endure almost anything for it, the lure
of greatness, the shiny hook
upon which adulation squirms.

The young man in the jeans and white T-shirt
has it, the chiseled dark glamour,
the allure of those
who resist being loved.

The women are many and various,
the trumpet's charismatic notes
sliding into their ears like promiscuous tongues.

Chet Baker looks down while he plays,
speaks little, smiles less.
He is a Gabriel for sinners,
a corrupt angel resisting rescue.

But they all try to save him, the women.
They try.

8.

After prison Chet Baker is Chet Baker.

No closed circle, no straight line.

The mistress eventually becomes the wife,
bears him three children.

Many years from now at his funeral
a vase of white roses
will suddenly and inexplicably shatter,
strewing flowers and broken glass
at her feet.

Nature's Response

The world poses.

We pose within the world.

The complacent birds fly off,
don't look back.

Precept

To focus on not focusing:
sometimes this is the answer,
sometimes not.

Remember: all that is placed in water
either sinks or floats.

You are your own forest,
and all the green shimmering
and all the darkness.

What gathers in the margins
of your invisible life
is depleted and replenished
as time, in its alternating current
of hope and hopelessness,
moves you.

Look it in the eye:
the horror and the wonder
that is transience.

Where there is fear,
celebration cannot enter.

Eliot Simultaneously

The essential advantage for a poet is not to have a beautiful world
with which to deal: it is to be able to see beneath beauty and ugliness;
to see the boredom, and the horror, and the glory. —T. S. Eliot

Imagine T. S. Eliot
walking west on Bloor toward Bay,
his serious eyes
hat-shielded from the late afternoon sun,
the autumnal city
treacherous around him, the banker poet
in his waistcoat and newly polished shoes.

Text, for him: a block of type on a pristine page,
its black-and-white clarity a steady reassurance, something
to be counted on.

The world is not a stable place—was it ever so?
Time intrudes, always, and every age
is troubled in its own way.
(And let's not forget history's perpetual repetition.)

In this world with words for everything
and an understanding of nothing, Eliot
carries his briefcase of classical complications,
works his way forward, traditionally purposeful
in his peculiar greatness.

* * *

Rome, 1926. Michelangelo's *Pietá*.
Eliot falls on his knees, converts
to a new form of God,
conventional drama.

It is the year of gin and madness,
the former his, the latter his wife's.
He compares his life to a bad Russian novel, struggles
as he approaches forty
to cope with the world's tremendousness,
to crack the code of his own insurgent heart, volatile
beneath the fastidious mask of its routine social beating.

He forays into literature
on a plank of contrived neutrality
which he himself does not trust.
How to be objective about the buried life?
What price excavation?

* * *

There are things we never get over
even after we have forgiven,
even after we have been forgiven,

even after we have moved beyond forgiveness
to almost forgetting.

Eliot marshals the forces of opacity, the sum
of his various disappointments.
He provokes an arid euphoria that will linger for decades
undeniable in its tenacity.

His greatest fear: inertia.
Better to do wrong than nothing.

We hear him stammer a longing
(for what, he doesn't know).

An uncomfortable man,
an austere man,
a somber communicant.

A man immersed in his detachment,
detached from his immersion,
the paradox poet of the suit-and-tie soul
who knows that the past is never quite past
and all that was is continuously recognized.

And yet a man who despite his measured passions
attempts love in his own way.

ad nauseam   *ad infinitum*

The world-weary words shoved
into the closet of irrelevance,

turning and returning in their boxy darkness.

Yet he perseveres: with spoon after spoon stirs the days,
throws down his glove, hoists the pen.

So think of him there
at the corner of Bay and Bloor.
Think of what survives
and does not, in every conscious moment
memory and hope eliding.

And the one true command:
do not abstain from living.

Urban Hike

As we approach the viaduct,
you notice the backpack
directly in front of us
on the sidewalk.

A bomb or a jumper, you say,
not quite joking.

In seconds we reach it,
the ominous backpack.

You lean over the railing,
are thrown back
by what you see.

Don't look, you say,
and I understand
before you say the words.

Soon people surround us.
Nothing draws a crowd
like a public death.

It won't be in the news though.

Not a good idea
to give people ideas.

Bridge

In memory of Dorothy Farmiloe

I remember it
from my first visit to your apartment,
your painting
of the Ambassador Bridge, the vivid arch
pulled across the river
by your strong brush strokes
to that foreign other side
somewhere over and beyond.

I was seventeen
and looking to travel.

The painting took hold that day
and didn't let go.

It was a gift you gave me
like so many others
you didn't know you were giving.

Teaching

A student fails an assignment.
I invite him to my office to discuss it.
He arrives contrite and droopy-eyed,
ready to drop the course.

When I ask what happened, why
so many errors, so many confused sentences,
he tells me that his father was diagnosed last week
with cancer, and his fiancée
is in court fighting her abusive ex
for sole custody of her son.
Her ex's best friend fondles
the four-year-old every time he visits.
So far the law has not been helpful,
and home is an eight-hour drive away.
There is no money. He is on the verge of quitting.

Have you eaten today? the mother in me asks.

No, he says, and in that word are all the words unsaid.

Have lunch, I say,
pulling a bill from my wallet.

He starts to cry.
I look away to shield him,
hand him a Kleenex.

It is the least I can do.
It is all I can do.

And now to write this poem
whose price is his suffering.

Consequences

What is taken away in childhood
is hard to retrieve.

The boy of twelve
laughed off the dance floor
at a junior high dance
refuses to dance again,
not even years later
with his wife
in the privacy of their living room.

Because of this, the wife
(who loved to dance)
has no chance to,
in time loses
her own sure footing.

Becomes hesitant
with her next partner
who assumes
she doesn't like to dance.

Eventually
no one is dancing.

Wedding Video

As a gift
you film your friend's wedding.

It is August in the Thousand Islands,
sky and water flashing
on the bride's white, the groom's linen.

You and the camera everywhere:
ubiquitous collaborators
shaping the altar pilgrimage
into a sequence of moments,
the ritual record.

Years from now
it will be what you saved
that will bring them
back to themselves — promising bride,
promising groom — to this day
of vowing to each other.

And this I wish for you:
that one day
you will step from behind the camera,
a man turning
toward the woman he loves,
someone else behind the camera
recording love
with such love.

Motherhood

The road takes me
through the Tuscan countryside,
its postcard cylinders of hay
scattered among the cypresses,
the sun-sweetened fields
honey-gold and light-blessed.

I consider the ways of loving:
remember, imagine.

In every cathedral
I shamelessly summon the angels,
marshal the forces
to birth your happiness.

Anchovies

My sister remembers
the anchovies of our childhood,
two neat rows of salty circles
each curled around a caper
and resting in oil in the small rectangular tin.

We speared them with toothpicks,
she, our brother and I,
a New Year's Eve treat handed down
from our parents' cocktail world,
a bond among siblings.

She eats them still,
loves the rich mouth-burst
strong as Mediterranean heat in summer
and so unlike
the cold domestic landscape
we call adulthood.

I Speak With My Mother

I knew even as a child
that I couldn't love you, didn't know how,
and that you couldn't teach me.

Strange that here in my father's house
it is you I think of
as I long for daybreak,
the hopeful light of it, for it is spring
and the hesitant leaf-buds
are about to burst, sun-coaxed,
into green.

Have you ever truly known green?

The last time we spoke
you had just returned
from a walk by the morning lake.
Said you liked the early sun, the beach unpeopled,
the water calm in its neutral tenderness.
Actually, what you said was: *I like it when it's quiet.*

The light, you said, *was beautiful.*
Beauty is a story you tell yourself when you are brave.
I could tell you'd had a courageous morning.

About the night I did not ask.

Border Magic

The moment between touching
and not touching.

The space between reason
and the vagaries of love.

The fine line between ripening
and rotting.

Morning Birds

She stands at the window, watches
the morning sky open over the summer lake.

Watches as it becomes once again
the expected blue.

And, as every morning, there are the birds,
flying low, skimming—almost—the water.

From left to right they move across the page of her vision,
a row of feathered words, if only she could read them.

For a moment she closes her eyes.
It will be a blinding hot day.

Lake Poem

When the winter comes, the lake
resists freezing, its deep centre
a refuge for old life.

Destiny. Destination.

She reads
the fallen branches in the snow,
dark hieroglyphs.

This is what the water says:

Cross the distance
that only love can create
and only love can vanquish.

In the end
she opts for success in one place
by failing in another.

Animal Instincts

The lion's lackadaisical feasting.

The wolf's eye for weakness.

Your fiercely primed mistrust.

Where the Year Takes Us

So much has died this year.

Now, winter solstice:
shortest day, longest night,
and once again
a distance between us.

This too shall pass, and that and that.

There is nothing but the passing,
time trapped in melancholy squares
on calendar pages torn off one by one.

There is no reprieve from missing you.

The Schrödinger Principle

Between the knowing
and the not knowing:
a momentary gap—
the cusp—the edge—
the tightrope teeter—to fall
or not to fall.

This is the realm
of the undecided,
the not-yet-claimed,
the so-far-unobserved.

In this
middle place of possibility
(which some call fate)
we meet, and wait
for the outcome of us.

And Still

And still,
despite the carrion fear
the skin's fragile surface
invites love, says
Now. Please.

Persistence

Sneer and smirk, and call me mad
but always I will side with love
and always I will choose.

Despite the billion chattering screens
and time, which is on no one's side,
I persist in all I cannot prove.

Naïve, some say, to hold to faith
in days of war-fire reckoning
but show me days that were not so.

Within this truth love does exist
and wholeness still engenders grace.
I will choose, and so it is.

On the Other Side

On the other side
of truth
there is another
and another.

I will never know
whether I've chosen
misery
or happiness.

What It Is

It is the secret that stars carry, and the sun,
and anything that burns.

It is the piercing red of geraniums in summer,
the smell of ancient stones in the heat.

It is mazarine sky and water-polished stones,
the broken light of rainbows.

It is stupor and it is imperfection,
the energy of shadows.

It is the tiger sniffing the breeze
behind the curtains of your gracious life.

It is all that is galvanizing and sincere,
the exultant collapse of silence.

It is destiny's calligraphy drawn by angels,
the unconsummated strangers in all of us.

We Search

We search all our days for the triumph
of arrival, our mysterious hearts
certain that arrival is impossible.

We scatter the crumbs of our thoughts
across the earth, our hungry parent.

We give and we receive,
sometimes more than the other.

At our root much lies dormant, and
if we were aware, this would frighten us.

And this too: our affinity
with the buoyant helpless clouds.

In the end, which seas, which skies?
By what growth will we be overcome,
by what surprise sheltered?
Which suns will light us, which stars?

Around us the bounty of endlessness revels,
holds us free.

What we choose: a belief in choice.

It is thus that we become substantial and reduced,
and the humble glory strengthens.

Our children and their children make it their own,
and in this
something (perhaps joyful) survives.

Archeology

Exhibited:
the last citizens of Pompeii.

Buried for centuries
under hardened ash and pumice,
their life-to-death moments
have been caught in plaster,
cast into a haunting art.

Irony:
that what destroyed
also preserved.

As we stand
before them now,
their imprints
of mortality, shapes
of departure,
we remember them
by the spaces they left,
their sacred absences.

At the Villa Diodati, 1816

The reign of rain.
June on Lake Geneva
in the Year Without a Summer
when volcanic ash winters the world.

From room to room the exiles stalk
the rhythm of the rain.
Byron, Shelley, the doctor Polidori,
Mary Godwin, her stepsister Claire—
an unholy quintet
in the restless fog, relentless chill.

The sky electrifies them,
galvanizes their hunger
into a panther lunge at words.
It is words they feed on,
words they need.

At night
they gather in the drawing room,
tell ghost stories, thrill each other
with fear.

When Mary wakes from dreams
of flesh and sparks, she births a monster
on the page.

Her ink flows
charged with fate and focus

like the perfect mind of lightning
when it strikes twice
in the same place.

And throughout it all
the rain rains.
There is no reining in the rain.
It beats on
like the hooves of a thousand horses.

Nature's forces both,
Mary and the rain.

Byron's Grotto

1.

In Portovenere
below the Church of San Pietro
Byron sits musing
in the Grotto Arpaia, watches
the waves move and move.
Their never-stillness captures him,
arrests his attention.

Soon he will swim
the 7.5 kilometres to Lerici
where Shelley awaits him
in nearby San Terenzo
behind the whitewashed walls
of the Casa Magni.

They will talk of God and fate,
the profligate winds, incorrigible sea.

Irreclaimable, the both of them,
admitting to nothing
but an allegiance to words.

2.

Two centuries later
the afternoon sun bronzes the blue

in Byron's grotto,
the seductive light lulls and lulls.

Ingenuous acolytes, we are beckoned
by the unpredictable water,
its capricious variations, hidden debris.

Can almost hear the poet whisper:
paradise is less than freedom,
and all that dreams also grieves.

Legacies

We do not remember days, we remember moments.
—Cesare Pavese

All three will die far away from home:
Keats in Rome
in a room by the Spanish Steps,
Shelley in a storm-pummeled boat
in the Gulf of Spezia,
Byron in Missolonghi
fighting for Greek freedom.

Consumption, drowning, fever—
death never romantic.

Best to think of them in life, the poets,
to remember them in their particulars.

Look: there is Keats
sprinkling pepper on his tongue
to intensify the flavor of his cold claret.

And over there: Shelley, grown tired
from his incessant reading, shifts
from his chair to the floor
where he sleeps on the sunlit rug
like a cat.

And there: Byron, in his Venetian *palazzo*,
lifts the quill from the page
to admire the peacock that preens past him.

Moments are mirrors, together reflect a life,
its sparkle-dance in continuous motion
like light on water.

Look too at your own reflection
in the granite kitchen counter.
See there the immutable rhythm
of everything becoming, passing away.

Byron Addresses His Last Mistress

My blood is all meridian, I once wrote,
and so it is, will always be.

Other loves were feral and unchecked,
but not so this.

Though the night approaches,
it is not time for remembering yet.

Give me your hands,
and I will hold back the words.

Mia cara, we will take our solace
from the silence and the stars.

Cerasi Chapel

In the corner shadows
the brooding Caravaggios wait.

Slip a euro in the slot
and—surge of surprise—
they are illuminated.

On the left
The Crucifixion of St. Peter,
on the right
The Conversion of St. Paul.

Consider: over 400 years ago
the artist stood exactly here
appraising his creations, the spew
of his own torment on the canvas.

Wounded flesh, earthly terror,
the suffering
of what is insufferable,
but most of all
the violence of light
as it strikes darkness.

The Artists

The artists
have always dared
to look for God.

Embedded in the storied walls
of mosques and synagogues,
temples and cathedrals, their souls
are fused with seeking.

The divine absences
do not deter them.

The wars of the pious
do not deter them.

The words of the fear-mongers
do not deter them either.

The artists refuse
to be deterred.

A frisson of faith
in a moment of colour,
redemption
in a tile.

These are the ways of creation,
and rapture
is never neutral.

Theatre of War

In every century
a new stage for the same drama.

Weapons evolve.
Planes go down.
Ships sink.

People take to the streets
in revenge or refuge.

Witness the beheading
of mercy and reason,
afterward
the loud shock of silence.

Every player has a role—
bystander, victim, perpetrator.
Triangle of collusion.

What never changes:
the outcome depends
on which wind prevails
and what you consent to.

Television News

Brutality muted by the touch of a remote,
the framed images vanquished by that same touch.

The word *remote* itself morphed into a noun,
a tool of distance.

Everything said before and said better
by those who have earned the right to grieve.

Words at best an expression
of what in safe beds is merely gratuitous empathy.

Yet all I have are these words, these words, these words:
an offering of prayer.

Everything Happens Elsewhere

So tell me:
how do you feel on a deserted street
at midnight?

The Fear

Each morning the fear lies on your chest,
waits to be fed.

The moment you open your eyes
you feel its fleshy heaviness.

Where you are: the ever-present.
The only place: here.

Around you people vanish.
Friends, strangers.

You try to ignore the signs,
everywhere
nature in revolt or in hiding.

From the open window
sunlight falls upon you,
undeterred benediction.

Your mind noses for meaning
the way a dog sniffs for spring.

What do you deserve
when there are only sewers?

What can be salvaged?

What Remains

What remains (if we are lucky)
is what we started with:
water, trees, the unyielding sky.

Not the virtual fortunes or abstractions,
beguiling as they are.

On Easter Island 887 stone heads
stare down time, monumental reminders
that art might survive.

But worth remembering also:
there is no hubris in the stars.

The Women

The women have always been here.

They tend to the graves of those they've loved
and of those who have been strangers.

They understand
the art of wells and ditches,
the way things form, disintegrate
at the same time.

They know
the warp and weft of weaving,
the necessity of food, its preparation.

They welcome the cleanse of burning.

Birth is their faith,
growth their unconscious language.

When they speak it, sparks
find safety in the wind.

Sea Silk

Delicate as a spider's web, byssus,
fabric of pharaohs and emperors,
shimmers in the sun like gold.

Only one woman left
who knows the sacred art of it,
how to harvest, spin and dye
the silky filaments of the *Pinna Nobilis.*

A dozen dives
into the Mediterranean,
one gram gathered, the silk
never sold, only given,
a gift of the sea.

She says that selling it
would be like selling
the flight of an eagle,
instead gives it
to those who come in need,
the outcasts, the poor,
the young women seeking
blessings on their marriages.

At night she thinks of them all
as she chants
in ancient Sardinian and Hebrew,
prays for what has been,
what will be.

Caregiver

A constellation of endings,
loss after loss.

You are supposed to be happy.

It is summer, after all.

Yet it is hard to watch
history repeat itself,
the same
but never the same.

And it is always personal
though from a distance
we don't admit this.

Every day
you watch over your mother.

Every day
you watch over your sister.

On your watch
love never falters.

Another Hour Passes

Another hour passes, another day.
I grow older and less wise
having recognized that wisdom
is merely a concept that the young
wish for their future.

Lately, I have been undeveloping.
Not an easy task, but as necessary
as taking out the garbage.

It involves returning to the heart
and a semblance of stillness.
Innocence doesn't enter into it.

Unhitching

Break out
of your bones
and open to them,
the wet sidewalks
and their leaf tattoos,
the fractal beauty
of the fall cornfields,
their jagged edges
of growth.

Feel the reprieve
below
your buzzing consciousness,
the deep knowing
that comes
with unwilled attention.

Become
your very self,
unprecedented.

Despite What I Read in the News

The birds
are eloquent
in the festive trees
and my heart,
riffing on their songs
of yes and gladness,
plays spring.

How She Breaks

You're at a loss:
what to do
with the clay portrait
now that the subject
(having imagined herself
differently) has disowned
your depiction.

For days
the heavy head occupies
a corner of your studio,
waiting.

Until it strikes you
with irresistible certainty:
you will be an agent of change,
the arbiter of her transformation.

And so
you carry her to the high porch
above the concrete driveway,
do not pause before you let her fall.

Know that it is not that she breaks
but how
that will matter.

Sophia

Ripped from the earth she bares
her heart-root and jagged edges, wears them
as the trees wear their leaves,
preordained and vivid.

Once moist and malleable,
she's now been fired
into a welcome hardness.

But don't be fooled:
it is her eyes that are your master.

Although they ask you questions,
they already know what they know.

You Ask

Art is a form of consciousness.
—Susan Sontag

1.

From one fraction of an instant: all.

The spontaneous birth of light, the only reality,
and that is what love is.

2.

It begins with the first art—handprints
stenciled on a cave wall, the artist pushing
left palm against rock
while the other hand paints around it,
once, twice, a third time.

Stencils of existence: *I am here.*

Life, so large and small simultaneously,
invents itself. From a few roots,
an entire forest.
This is the way of creation.

3.

Each year, cell by cell, you replace yourself.

Every seven years you are not who you were.

You look up, pretend
there is an *up* in the universe.

You heed yourself, the I of the eye.
Struggle forward in your circular pilgrimage,
your perpetual ardent reaching.

You go where attention takes you.
With your eyes you reach into the world.

4.

What you find: everything spins.

Time and you merge,
a fusion of fusions.

Within the infinite, such diversity,
the miracle of one, yet no separateness.

What moves your soul
is what calms the anxious leaves
as they shift to meet the storm.

What you find

is the illusion of finding.

Eventually you understand
that everything conspires to love.

5.

Focus: what continues
is what you allow.

Within the nearness and the farness,
responsibility grows.

It is to yourself
that you must make the serious promise:
pledge, above all, to live.

This involves more than breathing.

6.

You ask: what proof?
You ask: why poetry?

Because each word ignites like a tiny sun
and light changes everything.

Because change is a beacon
and what is important
will in time find you.

7.

You did not plan to hold the pen
or write what you did.

You did not wish for the onus of knowledge,
the kind that comes from the Third Eye and the Muses.

What you wanted was to be
a resting body between the crisp white sheets of your childhood,
sheets that smelled of spring because they had dried on the line.

What you wished for was innocence,
your heart a whole possibility unbroken by loss.

But there is no rest, only invisible motion,
everything moving even when it appears
most absolute and still.

What is it that you need then
from the time that is left—
a minute or decades or a point in between?

Is there a god who can grant you abstinence from asking?

Consider the luminous immensity, space and time
expanding into new dimensions, the unsolvable mystery
of your hand in the world.

Fathom yourself into the vastness which holds the stars.

Notes and Acknowledgements

A note on the cover image: Stephen Orlando photographs movement (in this case a kayaker paddling across a lake) and in so doing, photographs the passing of time. His work is visual poetry. It is not Photoshopped.

"Circles and Lines"—Various factual details of Chet Baker's life can be found in *Deep in a Dream: The Long Night of Chet Baker* by James Gavin (Chicago: Chicago Review Press, 2002).

"At the Villa Diodati, 1816"—When Mount Tambora in Indonesia erupted in 1815 it cast enough ash into the atmosphere to block out the sun and created colder than normal temperatures in Switzerland among many other places. Hence 1816 became known as the Year Without a Summer.

"Sea Silk"—The woman in this poem actually exists. Her name is Chiara Vigo, and the poem was inspired by an article about her written by Max Paradiso.

"Unhitching"—The title comes from the beautiful final paragraph that closes *Tristes Tropiques* (1955) by Claude Lévi-Strauss: "...the possibility, vital for life, of *unhitching*, which consists ... in grasping, during the brief intervals in which our species can bring itself to interrupt its hive-like activity, the essence of what it was and continues to be, below the threshold of thought and over and above society: in the contemplation of a mineral more beautiful than all our creations; in the scent that can be smelt at the heart of a lily and is more imbued with learning than all our books; or in the brief glance, heavy with patience, serenity and mutual forgiveness, that, through some involuntary understanding, one can sometimes exchange with a cat."

"Wedding Video" and "Motherhood" are for Brendan McCarney.
"How She Breaks" and "Sophia" are for Constance Rennett.
"Precept" is for Jane Neily Mallay.
"Caregiver" is for Darlene Hareguy.

"Circles and Lines" is dedicated to Diane Vavra.

"You Ask" was published in the Fall 2015 edition of *The Windsor Review.*
"What It Is" was published in the Dec. 2015 edition of the *Literary Review of Canada.*

A special thank-you to Patricia Abram for her insightful comments not only on the final form of this particular manuscript, but for her unflagging enthusiasm for my poetry over the past twenty years.

And, as always, my deepest thanks and appreciation go to Luciana Ricciutelli for her unwavering support of my work.

Photo: Constance Rennett

Eva Tihanyi teaches at Niagara College and divides her time between Port Dalhousie (St. Catharines) and Toronto. *The Largeness of Rescue* is her eighth volume of poetry. She has also published a collection of short stories, *Truth and Other Fictions.* www.evatihanyi.com.